FARM ANIMALS

PIG

Katie Dicker

W

FRANKLIN WATTS

LONDON • SYDNEY

 An Appleseed Editions book

Franklin Watts
First published in Great Britain in 2017
by The Watts Publishing Group

© 2013 Appleseed Editions

Created by Appleseed Editions Ltd,
Well House, Friars Hill, Guestling,
East Sussex TN35 4ET

Designed by Hel James
Edited by Mary-Jane Wilkins

ISBN hardback 978 1 4451 5109 0
Dewey Classification 636.4

A CIP catalogue for this book is available from the British Library

Photo acknowledgements
l = left, r = right, t = top, b = bottom
title page Tsekhmister/Shutterstock; 3 iStockphoto/Thinkstock;
4 IA98/Shutterstock; Mark William Richardson/Shutterstock;
6 iStockphoto/Thinkstock; 7 jadimages/Shutterstock; 8 Ru Bai Le/Shutterstock;
9 Tsekhmister/Shutterstock; 10 iStockphoto/Thinkstock; 11t Anders Moden/
Shutterstock, b Nigel Paul Monckton/Shutterstock; 12 Hemera/Thinkstock; 13
John Marquess/Shutterstock; 14 Yu Lan/Shutterstock; 15 iStockphoto/Thinkstock;
16 tratong/Shutterstock; 18 Hemera/Thinkstock; 19t iStockphoto/Thinkstock,
b lafoto/Shutterstock; 20 MaxPhoto/Shutterstock; 21t IbajaUsap/Shutterstock;
r Graeme Dawes/Shutterstock, b iStockphoto/Thinkstock;
22 Hemera/Thinkstock; 23 John Foxx/Thinkstock
Cover Tsekhmister/Shutterstock

Printed in China

Franklin Watts
An imprint of Hachette Children's Group
Part of The Watts Publishing Group
Carmelite House
50 Victoria Embankment
London EC4Y 0DZ

An Hachette UK Company
www.hachette.co.uk

www.franklinwatts.co.uk

Contents

My world

I am a pig. I live on a farm with lots of other pigs.

Oink!

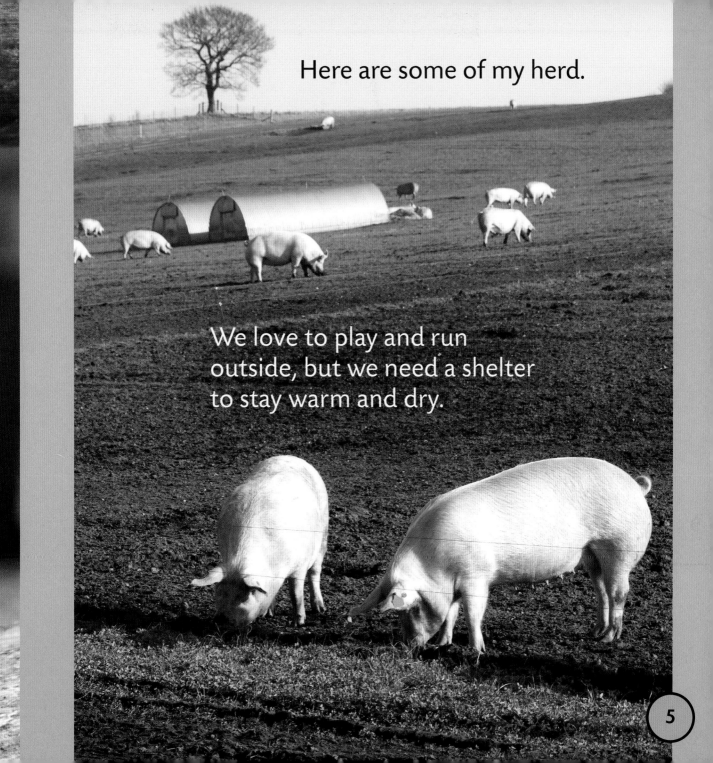

Here are some of my herd.

We love to play and run outside, but we need a shelter to stay warm and dry.

Keeping cool

In the hot summer sun we need a shady place to rest.

Pigs get hot or cold very easily, depending on the weather.

Rolling in the mud is another fun way to keep cool!

Pigs can't sweat so they have to find other ways to cool down.

My nose is called
a snout. I have an
excellent sense
of smell.

Sniff!

Our feet are called hoofs. We have four toes on each hoof.

Most pigs are pink, brown, black or white.

On firm ground, pigs walk on just two of their four toes. It looks as though they are walking on tiptoe!

Teeth and ears

Male pigs (boars) have long canine teeth, called tusks, which stick out from their mouth.

Some wild pigs use their large tusks to fight and to dig for food.

A pig's tusks grow all through its life.

Pigs have pointed ears that sometimes hang down.

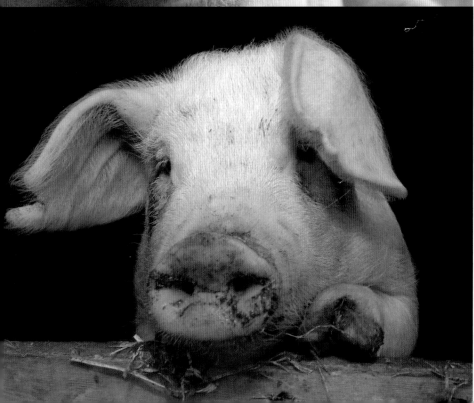

Pigs grunt and squeal. When they hear these noises, they know how other pigs are feeling.

Who looks after us?

The farmer cleans our shelter
and gives us fresh straw to lie on.

From the day we are born we have health checks.
A vet visits to trim our tusks and hoofs.

Time to eat

We eat grain, which is full
of the goodness we need
to grow big and strong.

Snuffle

I use my snout
to find other
food. If I'm
lucky, I may
smell a snake
or a worm!

Snuffle

15

Pigs and piglets

Female pigs have babies, called piglets, about twice a year. A boar is used to breed them.

There are usually about ten piglets in a litter.

Farm produce

Pigs are farmed for their meat,
called pork, and for their leather.

When pigs reach
a healthy weight,
the farmer takes
them to market.

Sausages, bacon and ham also come from pigs. Pork is sometimes smoked to give the meat more flavour.

Cooking pork on a barbecue is one way to add a smoky flavour.

Pigs around the world

Gloucester Old Spot, England

Farmers in countries all over the world keep pigs. Some pigs live in the wild and others are kept as pets! Here are some of the different breeds.

There are more than 70 different types of pigs around the world.

Wild boar, Europe

Pot-bellied, Vietnam

Kunekune,
New Zealand

21

Did you know?

Pigs are very hungry creatures. They eat two or more kilos of food every day, or about a tonne every year.

In Australia, a sow once had a litter of 37 piglets.

Pigs can squeal so loudly they can hurt your ears. The noise they make can be louder than a chainsaw!

Pigs are clever animals and can be trained easily.

Useful words

boar
A male pig.

canine teeth
Pointed teeth at the side of the mouth.

herd
A group of animals that live together.

leather
A material made from the skin of an animal.

litter
A group of babies born to an animal at one time.

Index

Websites

www.animalcorner.co.uk/farm/pigs/pig_about.html
www.kidcyber.com.au/topics/animals/pigs/
www.ncagr.gov/cyber/kidswrld/general/barnyard/pigs.htm
www.onekind.org/be_inspired/animals_a_z/pig/
www.sciencekids.co.nz/sciencefacts/animals/pig.html